I Hope I Find the Wind

Terry Focht

Poems and Reflections

Editor-911 Books

Copyright © 2022 Terry Focht

All rights reserved.

Editor-911 Books in St. Louis, MO, USA

Contact the editor and author at www.editor-911.com for permission to reprint or use a portion of the book for educational purposes.

ISBN: 978-1-957366-09-8

Cover photo by Terrill Martinez

Cover design by Lindsay Prince

For Jan,
I opened my heart and found her there.

To my girls:

Jan

My wife
The love of my life
My Soulmate

Terrill

Our beloved, beautiful daughter
Who always looks for the good in every soul
Teacher, Writer, and Leader

Natalie

Our first beautiful granddaughter
Now a beautiful young woman
Great Spirit, Great Talent, Great Expectations

Elena

Our youngest beautiful granddaughter
Sweet, funny, artist
Bravest of us all
A Precious Gift from God

Blessed Gifts All

Praise for
I Hope I Find the Wind

"The first time I was on the phone with Terry Focht, getting directions to meet with him, he finished by saying, "Chuck, you can't miss me—I'll be the one that looks like me." It is with this kind of wit and charm and playfulness, amply evidenced in his previous collection *Random Acts of Thought* and his children's classic *Grandpa Street,* that Terry continues to endear himself to so many of us. Don't miss out on the opportunity to spend some time with Terry's latest offering, *I Hope I Find the Wind,* and his more serious side---the amazing self who crafts these very personal, heartfelt, timely poems and stories."

~Chuck Stringer, poet and songwriter

"Terry Focht's *I Hope I Find the Wind* is a book of poems and prose lifted by love – love of words, of the sacred, of family, and most of all, love for his wife, Jan. "I inhale your rhythm/ Old Heart/ Cadence of my life," Terry writes. Whether speaking of a brush with mortality, the pain of his childhood, the joy of his family, the distress of illness, or finding humor in small observations, Terry's immense heart shines through."

~ Pauletta Hansel, Cincinnati Poet Laureate Emeritus

CONTENTS

Perhaps 1

The Word Whisperer 3

A Small Child's Words 5

Big Turtle Creek 6

Bell Buckle Cafe 8

A Fractured Reality 10

I Must Run 14

Campfire 16

I Hope I Find the Wind 19

Grandma Briggs 20

Soaring 22

Truth and Lies 24

Hidden Passages 25

Her Prayer 26

The Light 28

Wondering 29

Footprints 29

Softly 29

Winter Children 29

A Being of Age 31

A Man of Many Miles 32

Blessed Be the River 33

I Close My Eyes So My Soul Can See 34

Better Together 37

We Are From 38

Simplicity 41

A Brave Heart	42
Hidden Heirlooms	43
Poetry Math	44
'40 Ford Sedan	46
Thinkin' About Stuff	48
Mommy	51
They Call Him P.A.	52
Rust Belt Kid	54
Arcadia Boulevard	56
A Family of Spring	58
We Ran into the Future Like We Knew the Way	60
A Precious Work of Art	63
Flat-Footed Dancin' and Turnin' in a Circle	64
Soul Crafting	68
Old Heart	70
Sit Down, Daughter	71
I Met God's Eyes That Day	72
Who We Are	75
Special Thanks to These Publications	79
About the Author	80
Other Books by the Author	82
About the Publisher	83
Other Books by the Publisher	84

Love and poetry need each other.

PERHAPS

How do words come to life?
Are they derived from
the creative spirit
we all possess?

What changes an idea
into something that
actually exists,

that has the potential to be shared,
to be joyful and vulnerable
at the same time?

Is it the courage one has
to put ideas down on paper,
to give ideas life
or
is it simpler than that?

Perhaps…there is a destiny for words.

My soul has awakened from the slumber of life.

THE WORD WHISPERER
For Pauletta Hansel

Somewhere in the sky
a murmuration
not seen…
        only felt

a treasure
for a gifted seeker

words on the wind
spiraling, floating
catching the foil

drawn to the warmth,
drafting among the clouds,
waiting for the poet

coming
to bring them light.

Her heart
reaches into the depth
of the intricately
formed patterns

beautiful shapes
twisting, turning, shifting
transforming
among the clouds

her mind wide open,
her soul sees and embraces
the murmuration,

words on the wind.

Terry Focht

To rejoice in other people's gifts and graces.

~From the *Book of Common Prayer*

A SMALL CHILD'S WORDS

From the beginning of time,
the prophets and poets
philosophers and great thinkers
have searched for the meaning of love.

They have looked to the heavens
and deeply into the mind,
embracing every feeling
encouraging great thought.

But only a few,
the truly blessed,
have discovered the simplicity of this truth,
in a small child's words,

Daddy, Daddy, Daddy.

BIG TURTLE CREEK

Deep down
in Jackson County,
where Mountains
and Blue Grass meet,
seems there's a creek
around every bend
and old Native American trails
to find your way.

Every summer
Uncle Moss and I
hiked those trails,
scouting for one more
fishin' hole.

Folklore says Daniel Boone walked here.

Cane poles and fishin' knives,
compass and canteen,
sleeping bag and fish stringer,
fresh dug worms and crawdads,
just about all a boy would need.

He taught me how to fish,
to scale and to gut,
attacking my fingers,
fish eggs and guts,
guts and worms,
fresh meat and guts.

"Be careful now,
those catfish will sting ya," he sang,
as I bravely and boldly
whacked off their heads.

I Hope I Find the Wind

The sun…too soon fading,
catfish sizzlin' on a stick,
fresh caught marshmallows,
campfire stories,
imagined calls of native drums and flutes,
of spirit dancers, in rhythm with the earth,
stars living just above the treetops,
dew from the darkening forest
settling on my sunburned skin.

BELL BUCKLE CAFE

Bell Buckle is the smallest town in Tennessee and ten minutes from nowhere at all. It is a historic railroad town from the Victorian period and has long been resurrected as a tourist destination. The drive to Bell Buckle from Nashville, Murfreesboro and Shelbyville is a drive back in time to a destination ripe with country history, farmhouses and Tennessee walking horses. Victorian homes dot the main street that resembles a location made for Hollywood. It appeals to visitors looking for a peek back into a quieter, simpler time.

Tucked away, in the foothills of history, you can feel the romance and occasionally, smell a pig roasting on the fire pit when you enter the outskirts of town.

You can visit its historic recording studio or one of the many antique shops or get homemade ice cream from a marble fountain and back-bar. In a tiny candy shop, you can partake of one of its treasures—big, delicious pieces of homemade fudge with walnuts or pecans on top. You can visit the old country store where there is a display, above the shelves, of Civil War clothing, some used and some never worn. Some were for small children.

If you're really lucky, you might even be in town for the Moon Pie Festival.

The place you *absolutely* do not want to miss is the Bell Buckle Cafe, where you step across its stone threshold, worn down by time, where the old, wooden screen door creaks of age, as it welcomes you in, and the savory odors assure you that you made the right choice. There are red-checkered tablecloths and creaky wooden floors, metal advertising signs on the ceilings, and a small, sacred stage with musical instruments at the ready. It's a stage where the likes of Merle Haggard and Vince Gil, Dolly and Reba, Lester Flat and Earl Scruggs and even Elvis might have sung and reveled with the customers. It's the stage where Willy Nelson and Waylon Jennings and many others might have tested new songs and sang old country favorites, where hoedown fiddles and banjoes came alive with the sunset. There is a historic photo gallery of many of the greats and not-so-greats of country music that stopped by for apple pie or lemonade.

There is an endless supply of flat fried biscuits and honey, Southern fried chicken, country-fried steak drowned in gravy, grandma's meatloaf, fresh caught catfish, fried green tomatoes, greens, and a mountain of mashed potatoes. There are bottomless glasses of lemonade and sweet tea, salads with strawberry vinaigrette, and homemade peach cobblers—just a few of the dishes that are served. There are pies of many fruits, chocolate cakes, red velvet cakes, and hot, steaming coffee. It's a place where there are always more sweet rolls, biscuits and gravy, and homemade bread…

Down-home feasts. *Every day.*

There are no strangers at Bell Buckle Cafe, only friendly folks and smiling faces, strawberries, apples, grapes and bananas, just a little something to cleanse your palate before the floor starts to vibrate, and the stage comes alive.

It's a place where you can have two desserts and not feel guilty and one more glass…

of the best lemonade you ever had.

A FRACTURED REALITY

Outside my fractured window,
a country gasps for air
trapped in a time of madness.

My mind scrambles
descrambles
rescrambles
the bits and pieces
of heaven and hell.
Outside our door
a broken, distorted reality

yet, a dark…literary feast

a gastronomic delicacy of
word and wit,
madness and irony,
perfectly spiced,
peppered and stirred
into a crucible of crazy,
seasoned with sarcasm,
ignorance, audacity
humor and heartache,
the truths, the lies
the news
the fake news
the fake government
the easily deceived
the elected cowards
telling their stories
their rationalizations

to the laughter deprived
occupants of our country.

This surreal…literary soup
boils over,
bitter with lies,
deception,
complacency, conspiracy
and downright stupidity

from the Whitehouse,
the federal government
and other mental institutions.

Terry Focht

Fill my heart with compassion.

Speak to me of love.

I MUST RUN

Open my eyes, Lord,
open them wider than ever before.
Put silver on my tongue
not to offend a single soul.
Fill my heart with compassion,
heighten my intellect.
Let me not miss
the sweetness or bruises.
Let my mind leap.
Let my spirit embrace every experience.
Let my tolerance reach new heights.
Let me not miss a single word
of man and angels sent my way.
Let the earth caress me,
speak to me.
Let nature teach me
the secrets I've missed,
where man has come and gone,
where angels dwell.
Speak to me of love,
of the mornings after,
of friends and places,
of people I've known,
of those hero mothers
behind each door.
There is *so little* time to pause,
I must run,
run to the Earth's experience,
run to the back of the line,
to the front,
collect the stories,
the thoughts, the feelings
of those less noticed,
of those winning the race,
of those in the run.

I Hope I Find the Wind

Speak not of sitting out the dance,
but of the fire of life before the fall,
Of birds and babies,
grandparents and children.
And when the time comes, Lord,
take my hand,
lead me to the mountaintop.
Let me see who I might be.
Let me bathe in your waters, Lord.
Take me home to your river,
take me home to thee.

CAMPFIRE
For Sherry Cook Stanforth

Night's beauty was arising
as the sun slowly descended
into the forest,
beyond the mountains,
perhaps,
to a secret place
only nature knows.

Blue evening shadows
danced in the fields
as the fire caller
warbled her invitation
for the storytellers to assemble,
singing the poetry
of evening's call.

I'll Fly Away...
filled the air,
like the voice of nature itself.

Our spirits, hearing it first,
were called
and stepped in time
to the melody.

Slowly we gathered,
taking our place
around the campfire.
Each accompanied
by our shadows,
to experience the secrets
of the night.

Anticipation was great
and joy grew,
as the circle filled.
It was a night for sharing.

What new feelings would arise
from this amber portrait?
What poetry,
what song,
what words
would visit?
What dance
would appear?
What declaration
would the shadows bring?

What secrets would be
unmasked this night?

Our voices rose,
toes tapped,
hearts were full
in rhythm with the night.

Each voice
privileged participants,
of a centuries old ceremony,
sharing our stories
around a crackling campfire.

Mountain poetry was in the air.

Terry Focht

Did we honor their souls?

I HOPE I FIND THE WIND

Who'll read the words
of the poet when he's gone,
when he captures the wind
that takes him far
beyond the clouds?

                Oh, my love,
                I will leave you my words,
                my heart,
                our memories.

Who'll read his stories,
listen to his heart,
when the time arrives
for his soul
to fly away?

                how many dances have we danced?
                how many times have our souls kissed?
                how many dreams did we share?
                how many tomorrows have you given me?

I hope I find the wind
to take me to always,
for it is there
I will dwell,

                waiting for the wind
                that brings you to me
                once again,
                where our eyes will meet,
                our souls become one.

                where I will hold your hand

      forever.

GRANDMA BRIGGS

"Ay, you're *a bit of a dumplin', you are,*" Grandma would say as she pinched both of my chubby, Irish cheeks and gave a pat to the ones at the other end. My cousins laughed as Grandma uttered, "Now be gone with yourselves. Out of me way. There's work to be done."

Great Uncle John would fiddle and jig under the bric-a-brac while the whole of the family scattered through the house, awash in the smells of Grandma Iona's feast.

"Tis fit for the heavens and the Lord above..." I was in awe of Great Uncle, a leprechaun of a man, and the Irish music he seemed to live. I tried to jig in his presence, but "it is too little ye are to know the steps. Soon, you'll be bigger enough and show us all."

My mom and her sisters were the selected performers in a symphony of merriment and clangs coming from Grandma's kitchen. Hugs and kisses seemed to be part of the ingredients of Thanksgiving. "A hundred thousand welcomes to all" was her greeting to each and all of the family.

Grandma's kitchen was a magical place where love was made in the shape of a pie, where pumpkin bread and hot apple cider would fill the air, welcoming the holiday, where turkey was the main attraction and rolls and potatoes would soon find their way to the dining table, along with sweet potatoes and green bean casserole. Fruit salad and cole slaw would brighten the oak with red and yellow, green and purple. Now just a *"drip and a drop,"* of cinnamon and powdered sugar dusting the top, to open our senses in preparation of a special banquet. Toasts were made with lemonade for the kids and Guinness for the adults. Bottoms up was called, and *"Everything was grand altogether."*

The cousins were running through the house as always…only this day, with bright, white shirts and tiny ties and brand-new britches for the boys and little Sunday skirts and bobby socks with patent leather shoes for the girls. Out the door and into the yard, where Grandma's roses were still alive and overflowing on the garden altar and giving off the last of their fragrance for the season.

Grandpa Perry, and all our uncles, listened to football or sat on the porch talking about shop and politics until a few of them came to the yard. They stood watching us like they were trying to protect us from life. They looked taller, standing out there. I was happy they came. I knew I was safe when they were around.

Great Uncle John fiddled like he was back home in Ireland or as if he was trying to bring Ireland home to us. Grandma had a small triangle in the kitchen where she played and sang my favorite song. "Soups on – come and get it."

SOARING

There is a place above the Earth

a place so high
that it soars above
thoughts and perceptions
restricted by Earth.

It is a place where my soul is free

where my song is poetic,
where my poetry is my song.

Deep, deep down in my soul.

TRUTH AND LIES

Dreams are made up.

They are fantasies of a body at rest,
subconscious eruptions of
truth, fear, and temptations.

They are of ecstasy
and the reality
of our every fantasy,

our most hidden
hopes and dreams.

They are who we are
who we are not,

who we would
hope to be, and
never want to be.

They are both truth and lies.

HIDDEN PASSAGES

Dreams can make you face your fears
or
even in the darkest of times,
can bring light into your life
laughter to your heart and
adventure to your soul.
They can lead you toward salvation,
they can make you fly.

Yet, in those hidden passages
deep, deep down
where truth and lies
dwell hand in hand,
where love and fear
fight for life itself,
the battle for each dream
to exist
goes on and on
into infinity.

HER PRAYER
A border child

Why are you here
looking my way?
Don't you know that I am gone?
Why do you sing for me
when I am lost in the shadows?

I left myself
long ago
lonely, alone, forgotten.
Yet, this day, *you see me!*

Now, I cry inside,
for I have missed the lullaby,
the caring eyes,
the smile,
my soul.

Now…
You have seen me,
our eyes have met,
I have felt your tender touch,
so painfully new.

Hold me close
'til the pain goes away.
Sing to me
as if I were here.

Hold my hand tight,
remind me how to feel,
to hope.
Pray for me.

Pray me out of the shadows.
Make me real.

Are you an angel?
Come back.
Make me real,
so that I may be found.

THE LIGHT

The sound of water
gushing, pulsating
as it journeyed through the forest
crashing against wooded obstacles,
yet in perfect rhythm,
chanting its cadence.

The 3D images were darker
than I wanted them to be.
My mind eventually joined my eyes,
drawn to a distant light
alone…near the center.
There were medical specialists
quietly talking,
cautious,
with careful words.

I realized that very moment
I was looking inside of her,
inside a human being,
inside her heart, where I have lived
for almost 60 years.

I had rushed her to the ER
just hours before.
Her pain was great.
Her breath was weak.

Her heart had failed.

The echocardiogram was alive
with the noise of the forest.

We concentrated on the light.

WONDERING
Can nature
and its creatures
hear their own song?

Can they see
their own beauty?

FOOTPRINTS
How many footprints
on winter's blanket?

Where are they going
 those
   footprints of children
 on nature's quilt?

SOFTLY
Winter speaks
a soft, white language,
every snowflake
 every tree
  every animal sings
the music of nature.

WINTER CHILDREN
Children
ask the questions
of winter,

I wonder where the snow begins?
Does the snow love the Earth?
Does the Earth love the snow?

Will it snow for Christmas?
Are there really
Angels
in the snow?

Terry Focht

Our most precious work of art.

A BEING OF AGE

As a being of age
I cherish the memories
of
how my life was derived.

As an old man
I have earned my history.

As a young man
I struggled
to find my treasure.

As a child
I was that treasure.

A MAN OF MANY MILES

On the journey to myself
I hear the echoes
of days gone by

to recall the many paths
through the circumstance of life.

I search for the child I once was,
the undisciplined disciple
of the customs of the world

a world far too full of rules,

all the things
that keep a child from himself.

As a young man
I looked for the feelings, the senses
grown distant along the way

the sighs, the cries
the laughs, the screams
the untethered joy of childhood,

my journey into my own complexities,
to the memories of my youth.

Will I seize the time *or* will it seize me?

I will pull the young boy of unencumbered thought
to the man of many miles,
of many accomplishments
of many ironies
of many hopes
still.

BLESSED BE THE RIVER

there is a place
  where the earth meets the sky
    ordained, by the Creator
    where the nectar
      of the heavens flows
        to the tributaries of life

      gifting the earth
      with life itself
      where all nature's creatures
      share its nourishment
    where all nature's creatures
seek its comfort

birthed by the clouds
  the winding river
    plentiful, with
      sweet drops of energy

        Sacred, those waters
          to the Native Americans'
          nature quests
            upon its waters
              "ohi – yo"
                great river
                  beloved, a gift
                    to
                      early pioneers

                we…
              so blessed
              by its presence
            broad and mighty
            peaceful and still

            blessed be our river
            a gift from above

            a confirmation
            assuring us
            we are home

Terry Focht

I CLOSE MY EYES SO MY SOUL CAN SEE

Which questions
dwell still,
inside myself,
eyes locked,
as I fall away?

What answers remain unclaimed?
Is my mind in pursuit of a greater dream?

Can I rise
or should I take another way?

My mind grows weary from
searching for answers
to those stoic questions
that pass through time.

I've listened to the shamans,
the men of great faith,
the levelheaded logic
of the intellectually ordained,
to the eternal whisper
of space, time, and place.

Do I escape into the night
leave behind
desire,
curiosity,
blame?

How much time still?
A little too close I fear

once, so far away,

how do I join myself
for the final journey?

I close my eyes
so my soul can see.

Terry Focht

A place where my soul is free.

BETTER TOGETHER

I am so exhausted
from the divisiveness
in our country.

Science and Religion,
Philosophy and History,
Art and Literature,
have often told us
we are part of
something *much greater.*

Maybe, just *maybe*
we *are* part
of something greater.

Just think what it would be like
if our political leaders
would wake up
and finally realize,
we are…*better together.*

Maybe it comes from something
deep down,
greater than the individual,
something extraordinary,
something spiritual,
perhaps…
              even divine.

WE ARE FROM

We are from the spirit of faraway places
        from the ancestral DNA
        of the heavens, the earth and the Father,
        the idea of man's being
        from the kindness of nature,
        that **allows** our existence.

We are from Heaven's melting pot
birthed from many nations,

From the destiny of man
        "Too many wars
        Victories and defeats
        Liberating life
        Wounded and deceased
        Honor and courage
        Undimmed by human tears."

We are from Native Americans
        Honored Peoples
        Revered Nations
        Nature's Keepers
        Spirit Quest

We are from The Great Migration
        Seekers of Freedom
        Men of Steel
        Women of Faith

From the giants of history
        Hearts of the pilgrims
        Curiosity and grit of
                the explorers
        Courage and stamina of early pioneers

We are from Jamestown
        Williamsburg and Plymouth
        The Nina, the Pinta, the Santa Maria
        The determination within man's soul

We are from the sun and the stars
        Mornings and midnights
        "Dawn's early light
        Twilight's last gleaming"

We are from boundless skies
        Purple mountains majesty
        Emerald green valleys
        Bounties of the fields
        Blessings in the air

We are from battles for Freedom,
        Equality
        Opportunity

We are from every nation
        Every color of man
        Hard worn hands
        Bent backs
        Sun worn skin
        Scars of bondage
        Scars…of…freedom

We are from the colors of our flag
        The Lord's Prayer
        Manifest Destiny
        Emancipation Proclamation
        The Pledge of Allegiance
        In God We Trust
        United We Stand…
        Divided we fall

We are from
        "The tired, the poor,
        the huddled masses
        yearning to breathe free"

We are the people.
We are the hopes of our children.
We are the land.
We are…
        America.

SIMPLICITY

In spite of man's way
of complicating
the uncomplicated

God's word
God's truth

is as simple
as
His love.

A BRAVE HEART

She stands Mighty
as the strongest tree in the forest,
physically and spiritually strong,
facing down her opponent
with her Brave Heart.

She has the courage of a lioness,
brave in every way,
the peace and intelligence of a bird
full of love and joy.
She has the hope and magic of a unicorn
filled with spirit and imagination,
the freedom and regal attitude of a horse
standing tall and confident.

She has the beauty and endurance
of a butterfly,
the loveliness of a flower.

She has raced with leukemia
and beat it to the finish line,
leaving it far, far behind.

She has won the race and
the future is hers.

She stands in the winner's circle,
full of grace and beauty,
surrounded by her family,
every member beaming with pride.

She has won…
She is eternally brave,
She is Elena!

HIDDEN HEIRLOOMS

In that secret chamber
deep in my soul,
deep down
where memories are found
where laughter dwells,
where love lives eternal
relives
again and again
those sacred words
of my grandfather,
the outright laughter
of my best friends,
the forever giggle
of my mother,
whispered words
of my love and I,
living the beauty
of man and wife,
the first song
of my daughter,
first dance
of my granddaughters,
deep, deep…
deep down in my soul.

POETRY MATH
an 8 by 8, for Richard Hague

The poetry master requested wisdom wrapped in eights,
it seems easier than it might actually be,
words gently burped like a mother's loving pat.
They're in there *somewhere,* dancing around my organs
stuck in my chest, growling like caged wolves.
I hear their desperate rumblings trying to escape.
I am just afraid the task done properly
might just kill me…by mathematical, literary gas.

Our most hidden hopes and dreams.

'40 FORD SEDAN
Inspired by Sherry Cook Stanforth's "App Too" poem

Don't ask me why the air smelled and even tasted a little *bitter* sometimes, why the sky was often a rusty gray, or why our black '40 Ford Sedan always looked dirty, no matter how often we washed it. It must have been all used up before Dad brought it home. We never had a new car as part of our family.

We lived in a tiny, white house my dad built on a street that looked like someone planted rows of seed, and they all popped up out of the ground one day.

It was after the war, and many neighborhoods had houses the size of some garages these days. It was the early '50s, and I was excited about the planes from Wright Patterson Air Force Base breaking the sound barrier right over our house. I would roll on the ground and pretend to shoot at them with my finger.

All the kids played War those days and Cowboys or Tarzan. I guess we thought pretending like we killed our best friend was fun. Tarzan had gorillas and snakes we could wrestle with "'til we killed 'em all." Best of all, we yelled like Tarzan until *Mom* yelled at *us*.

At school, in first grade, we painted with our fingers and one time with our feet. We took naps on the floor and played, "Duck and Cover" under our desks "because the atomic bomb might come, and if we weren't under our desk, we might get hurt."

Dad had been to the War and lost a lot of his hearing and found some nervous feelings he didn't know he had. PTSD had not been invented yet. I remember he got a VA disability check, every month, for nineteen dollars. Like most other vets, Dad worked in a factory, where just a little security was offered for many of the men without college or a high school diploma. It was the place they hoped they deserved and *knew* they needed in order to support their Rust Belt families, hoping and praying their children would have a better life.

Dad was a machinist and lost an eye early in his career. This changed our lives substantially. Money was soon a problem; health care was a problem; dental and eye care was a problem. Yelling, anxiety, and discord were like members of our family. Mom cried too often. I was too young to understand the kind of pressure put on parents trying to take care of their family. I *did* know that *alcohol* was the head of *our* household, and it demanded obedience and loyalty. It got fed first and required almost constant attention.

Our '40 Ford Sedan was my imaginary friend. It seemed to always be smiling at me as I peeked at it through the wire rectangles of our fence. It took us to the market every Saturday for food. Grilled cheese and French toast were my favorites.

On Sundays, Mom made meatloaf, our gourmet dish of the week. Sometimes, on Friday night, Dad would take us to the Dairy Queen his friend owned, and I could get a hamburger. I only wanted sweet pickle relish on mine, my favorite. I had the back seat all to myself, and it was like my own little playhouse. They didn't have seatbelts back then, so my imagination and I were free to roam.

My favorite memory in that '40 Ford Sedan was when my mom gave me a present, and it wasn't even Christmas. It came in a long, round tube that had a Gabby Hayes steel fishing pole in it. I sat in the back seat that was all mine, smiling, laughing, and crying. I didn't know then that we were poor. I only knew that Gabby and I would soon go fishing in the grass, in our back yard—together.

THINKIN' ABOUT STUFF

Sometimes I rest my head on my fist and think about stuff.
I call those times…**"Thinkin' About Stuff."**

Stuff like the following:

Good News at the Funeral Home
I saw a beautiful cherry casket,
I wasn't in it.

The Secret of a Long Marriage
Always say, **"Yes, dear,"**
and you'll always be right.

The Worst Thing About Politics
Politicians

A Precious Gift
Upon retiring, I was given a most precious gift.
A gift so rare that it took my breath away.
I have never been more grateful for such a
wonderful, ongoing gift.
Naps.

Thank You, Lord
I needed to go to the bathroom,
everything worked.

The next one is the most important thing I ever wrote
I call it…**The Most Important Thing I Ever Wrote**

Cancer tried to destroy me.
It failed…
Let's eat!

**Good-bye for now. It's the middle of the day, and the sun
is shining brightly, people are at work, and it's time for my nap.**

To rejoice in a life of gratitude.

Terry Focht

Speak not of sitting out the dance.

MOMMY

I hear your voice…soft, gentle, soothing…you are coming to me.
My legs are kicking, my arms flutter at your voice.

I see you now…pretty and soft, happy and smiling.
My legs are jumping, my arms are flying.

You have come to me…will you touch me?
Will you sing me your song?

My little eyes race to keep up,
I see you now, my Mommy.

My little eyes so small and new,
I can only see my small, small world.

I see everything, I see you…my Mommy.
I hear everything, I hear you…my Mommy.

I feel you now…gently stroking me, lifting me into your arms.
I feel your warm embrace…I feel your love.
I feel everything, I feel you…my Mommy.

You tell me of your love for me,
I smile to tell you mine.

A tear from your eye lands on my face,
it is my tear now…you have given it to me.

THEY CALL HIM P.A.

His name was Perry Alexander Shinkle, and he was my hero. Grandpa.

He was a tall, thin man, over six feet. He had a long face that looked like a grandpa. He lost an eye as a machinist, but could see more than anyone I knew.

When he could no longer work as a machinist, he became president of the International Machinist Association, and I was proud. He always had time for me to go to the park and watch a ballgame while consuming too many popsicles. He showed me how to throw a curve ball even though I was too young to spell it. He always listened to me as I got older. He discussed life with me and made me believe that I mattered.

Most of all, we listened to the Reds.

From sitting on his lap as a small child, while he sang "Ole Suzanna" and I played with his extremely long earlobes, to the day I was the starting pitcher on the All-Star team, he was always there for me.

I saw his reaction, as I hit one over the left field hill and over the backstop of the diamond below. It took a while to recover the ball. I almost burst with joy, for no one had ever been to one of my sporting events, which later on became many. But he was there on our special day.

He had TB when he was young, and it left him with only half of a lung. He wasn't supposed to live, but God knew I needed him, and he lived a long life with only that half a lung. I would watch him in the morning when I spent the night, as he removed his glass eye to wash to begin the day.

It seemed as though life had unfairly taken away a part of him, but he was the most complete man I ever knew.

His name was Perry Alexander Shinkle, my hero. I love him for the time he gave me, for the man he was. I love him because he understood and wanted the best for me.

Then he died.

Because of his death, I could go to college. It was as if he knew.

He loved me once more.

RUST BELT KID
Inspired by Sherry Cook Stanforth's "App Too" poem

Don't ask me why I was brought home to a ramshackled shack with a washing machine on our tiny front porch. It was one of those hand crank jobs with rollers to squeeze out the excess water. Eventually, I would catch all my fingers and toes in those unguarded rollers. Sometimes, Mom used a washboard that I liked to strum like a guitar when she wasn't looking. Don't ask me why I would often stand in the tub, biting the edge of that imaginary guitar, bubbles and all. I wonder if that had anything to do with my neglected teeth and gums that ached too often.

I could look out the window of this tiny house on a hill, to the steps leading down to the factories and steel mills that gave off a putrid odor and filled the sky with rust, often turning the light of day into a night like darkness. We didn't have a car, so Dad would travel down those steps to his factory job, where he lost an eye and came home every day after that, with whiskey on his breath. Mom seemed to get a little older every time he did. Dad wore a black eyepatch back then, like a pirate, and would only take it off at bedtime, a gift from the factory that took half his sight and more of his self-esteem.

Dayton, Ohio, was widely known for its inventions and factories, but lessor known were the struggling parents trying to provide *and keep* food and shelter for their families. It was a factory town and raised families of steel and determination. Yelling, cries, and cursing were the anthem of this neighborhood.

My bones and muscles where cut from Rust Belt granite that pushed, pulled, and dragged me out of those hazy, painful, and lonely early days. Those days, when I had no friends to share my secrets, just Mom, who I clung to, and Dad, when the whiskey didn't love him first or put him asleep with his cigarette still dangling from his lip until Mom would put it out. To this day, I can still smell my early years, and they smell like loneliness and pain.

Don't ask me why some people supersede their dysfunctional childhoods, and why some people seem doomed to repeat them.

Grace? Tools and people placed in their paths? An inner drive? An inner knowledge that they were meant for something different?

We moved to a small, new house my Dad built with his VA loan before I started kindergarten, an area that seemed to be plentiful with veterans of World War II. Many were transplants from Appalachia, seeking fame and fortune at the factories, or at least a better life for their kids.

I seemed to grow more quickly than the rest of the kids, and all through grade school and high school, I wrapped myself in a protective armor of sports. I was spiced and colored by my Rust Belt bones of granite, my transplanted friends, and a covenant to **never** allow myself to *stand in pain*.

I learned the most important lessons of my life in Dayton, Ohio.

I learned that when someone or something
knocks you down,
you get back up.

I played all sports and conquered most, but excelled in Track and Field and knew it would be my path to new beginnings. It took me to college, and after ten years, full and part time, I began to learn who I was and how to succeed with a sometimes blessed, sometimes tortured, past. At the same time, my passion and compassion were growing for those *less noticed* and living with the dysfunctions of their own families.

I was becoming a Rust Belt teacher, an academically pruned, kind, caring, and sensitive specialized educator, down in the starting blocks, eyes and head forward, waiting for the sound of the starting gun, anxious to see where my life's race would take me.

ARCADIA BOULEVARD

I was all alone walking on the boulevard
where the crabapples grew,
my favorite way to school.
My mind was filled with stories
of the children that came this way before
of the time Buddy bit into one of those apples and
a worm popped his head out for his next bite.

There's Patsy's house, the prettiest girl in first grade.
I dare not look over
for fear of catching her eye and
having to talk to her,
or walk with her to school.

I think all the boys before me
looked her way hoping for a smile,
with dreams of holding her hand or
stealing a kiss.

I was much too shy to have such thoughts,
my face flushed just thinking about her.

Besides, today was the day for class pictures
and I was too worried about my cowlick.
I didn't want the other kids to say I looked like Alfalfa.
I peeked out of the side of my eyes at her house
pretending to laugh,
I jumped up and grabbed a crabapple
maybe to eat, maybe to throw.

I Hope I Find the Wind

Mrs. Trent marched us to the picture room,
where we lined up by height.
Patsy was beside me, but I dare not say a word.
My heart was jumping inside me.
The man said to smile and
Patsy grabbed my hand,
and held it tight.

It was soft and warm,
mine was shaking.
Now back on the boulevard after school,

I turned toward Patsy's house and smiled,
rubbed down my cowlick,
took the apple from my pocket
that I placed there on the way,
and ate every bite.
An apple never tasted so good.

A FAMILY OF SPRING

It was a Spring day, the sun revealed in brilliant presence.
Its rays descended upon the magnolia blossoms.
The willows glistened from the light.
Hearts were full…smiles were everywhere.

It was a warm, pleasant day in the country,
with all the beauty and glory of nature caressing the Earth.
A wedding was about to take place,
Heaven's grace was upon us.

A crowd had gathered,
a mixture of generations, a mixture of faiths
a mixture of beliefs.

People of all dress and description arrived to share in the joy of this happy event, on this day of love…all were one.

This special day was a celebration of the heart and new beginnings,
a new season had arisen,
the birth of a new family that would become one with nature.

We gathered in anticipation to see the joining of three souls.
The Bride and the Groom included their daughter in their ceremony.
Tears from our hearts gave way, at this gift of love.

A father's words would lead the way,
words of love and commitment flowed from the groom
to the bride and child,
words of love and understanding
mixed with tears of hope and joy from the bride.

Three rings were given,
man, woman and child were joined,
family and friends stood witness to this union of their souls.
A wedding had taken place. Heaven's grace was upon us.

We celebrated the event, the love, the joy, the inclusion of this day.
The sun shined brighter than before.
It was as if a confirmation from above had fallen upon this joyful
occasion.

Heaven's grace was upon us.

Terry Focht

WE RAN INTO THE FUTURE LIKE WE KNEW THE WAY

It was the early '60s,
teenagers and college kids alike
were looking to define themselves.

We were searching for our voice.
We were searching for our way.

We were not sure what we were doing,
but we knew we were destined to do it.

History tells us that every sixty years or so, there is a revolution.
It looked like our youth was claiming its turn.

Our youth marched, protested, sat down, and sat in.
We Ran into the Future Like We Knew the Way.

Our souls leaped, our souls cried.
We cried for the joy of the day.
We cried for the misery of the day.
We were searching for who we were,
and who we could be.

The days passed slowly…the times flew by.
We questioned everything.
Could we rise to the top by diving deeper?

It was the start, we thought, of a freer time,
a better time, a more loving time,
yet, a more rebellious time.

The establishment was at 6.4 on the Richter scale,
shaking in fear of what was coming.
The '60s were exploding.

There were thousands of causes and movements,
many worthwhile, many not,
many now forgotten,
some not forgiven.

Inclusion was gaining its place,
for many too fast,
for many too slow,

Oh God, for many too slow.

War loomed like a tornado in the background,
like a hurricane in our conscience.

There was a division in our country,
confusion in our brains,
volcanic eruptions to our peace.

Boys became men by going to war,
boys became men by not.

Many friends went to battle,
many came back,
too many did not.

Many never to be whole again.

Terry Focht

We lost a president.
The nation cried.
The world cried.

Everyone got older that day.
It was harder to breathe.

We were a nation divided…
A nation at war…

at war with our enemies,
our elders,
ourselves,
the establishment.

We were at war with war.

We prayed for Peace,
for the innocence of our youth.

We Ran into the Future Like We Knew the Way.

A PRECIOUS WORK OF ART

A new spirit of love
had entered the Earth,
a beautiful, intelligent heart

a daughter, ordained by God,
our most precious work of art.

God had shown
His Amazing Grace.

He blessed us with
His heavenly love,
the heaven of being
a mother and a father.

Terry Focht

FLAT-FOOTED DANCIN' AND TURNIN' IN A CIRCLE

Born I guess,
couldn't prove it by me,
not sure I was even there at all.
Thought I might have come from space
or radio, the kill
flattened on the road,

raised in Dayton, Ohio,
across from the Germans,
Dad's folks, or wild wolves,
hard to tell the difference,
too many razor straps and whiskey
Budweisers and bruises,
Stroh's and smokes
always smokes, for those folks
and Dad,
made me sick, forever.

Not sure why Mom stayed,
hope it wasn't my fault.

Uncle Moss, my favorite uncle
from Mom's people, of course,
always told me that Dayton, Ohio was
the capital of Kentucky or "Kentuck"
as he used to say,

somethin' about work and
I-75, the "hillbilly highway"
and a great migration.

I Hope I Find the Wind

Uncle Moss took me fishin',
sang me songs about that good ol' mountain dew
or riding a bicycle and landing in the grass with a sprocket
in his pocket and he'll never do it again
or she's got dimples on her "but" she is pretty.

He danced his flat-footed dance
and swung me in the air.
Put blades of grass between our fingers
as we made mountain music together.
He fiddled without a fiddle and
flat-footed danced some more.

I laughed and I cried,
still not sure he knew why.

I thought nobody knew
but he figured it all out, I think.
Uncle made me slingshots
gave me a BB gun
"don't shoot your eye out"
lingered in my head when Red Ryder and I
were often left alone.
He gave me pieces of leather for my 'magination, he said
and a knife much too big for me, with a spoon and a fork
a saw and hole punch to make
"growin' holes," in my belt he said.

He taught me how to shoot,
to play Kentucky knife games, still got a scar,
my favorite, 'cause it came from the
Kentucky knife he gave me.

He taught me how to gig a frog, pound it on the head,
grab its legs and cut 'em off, "Gotta make sure it's dead."

Mom always squirmed when they jumped in the skillet,
"Just hot enough, Maggie, you don't want'a hurt 'em,"
then Uncle Moss laughed, as he flat-footed some more.

"Gonna taste like chicken," Mom roared,
her big belly dancin', ashes falling to the floor.

He taught me how to fish, to scale, and to gut,
attacking my fingers,
fish eggs and guts, guts and worms, fresh meat and guts.
"Be careful now, those catfish will sting ya'," he sang,
as I boldly and carefully whacked off its head.

He laughed, with tears, when me and Ralph,
his sister's boy, became blood brothers, thanks to my knife.
We would hunt down the copperheads,
black snakes, and moccasins down by the lake,
hunt 'em all, with baseball bats…made us feel tall.
Ralph was Daniel Boone and I was Davey Crockett,
wouldn't think of givin' up our raccoon hats, even in the summer.

Uncle Moss was always my very own Kentucky Colonel,
flat-footed dancin' and turnin' in a circle.
Every summer for vacation, he took me to our mountains
where his home was mine, at least for the time.

I was always dreamin' I lived in Kentucky,
I knew it was there that my soul was born.

I was never so happy as with Uncle's arm on my shoulder,
his hands on my bruises talkin' things over.
I only hope he knew just how much I loved him for showing me
a place where the sun seemed to live at the top of the trees.

I close my eyes, so my soul can see.

SOUL CRAFTING

When will we see,
see enough
look deep enough?

When will we reach far enough,
touch our brothers in need
our sisters, our students?

Listen…
Are we listening?
Do we hear the rumbles of hunger,
the shallow breath of loneliness,
the pulsating cadence of pain and despair?

Did we see,
feel,
breathe deep enough,
listen close enough?

Did we look into every eye,
Deeply…deeply…deeply?

Did we celebrate their spirit,
caress their ideas,
did we feel their pain?

Did we give them breath…muscle?
Did we love them,
Care enough?

Did we celebrate their victories,
hear their stories,
listen to their songs,
see their tomorrows?

Did we hold their hands,
hold them tight,
pull them through,
lift them up?

Did we honor their soul?

OLD HEART

Listen to me,
old heart,
I hear your declaration

always with me

pulsating
vital
sanctioning
me to be.

I hear your secrets,
old heart,
keeper of first loves,
excitement of new adventure.

I feel your pain,
old heart,
guardian of heartaches,
deep in dark corners.

I hear your voice,
old heart,
quietly beating,
effortlessly

reminding me
you are there.

I inhale your rhythm,
old heart,

cadence of my life.

Be with me
until the end,
old friend.

SIT DOWN, DAUGHTER

Sit down, daughter, you've earned your rest today,
all your children are tucked away.

I see you working day by day,
carrying your family's burdens along the way.

I see you caring every day,
I see you caring every step of the way.

Put your feet up, child,
put your body to rest,
sit down, daughter, it's not a test.

Sit down, daughter, give yourself some time.
Sit down, daughter, let your burdens be mine.

Give your worries to me, my child,
you've *earned* this time of rest,
now it's time for me to bless.

I *know* you've become weary along the way,
sit down, daughter, you've earned your rest today.

Sit down, daughter,
your children are safe,
sit down, daughter, *you've earned* your rest today.

When your burdens are heavy, child – give them to me.
When your pains are *great,* child – give them to me.

When your eyes are full of tears,
I will replace them with my own.

Sit down, daughter, give those tears to me,
sit down, daughter.
You've earned your rest today.

I MET GOD'S EYES THAT DAY

I saw her running across the parking lot in a kind of *cloppity gate*, lifting her crutches and *pounding* them to the ground, like she was trying to win a prize for her effort. *Little did she know that she was the prize.* My life changed that day. *Destiny* was running my way, *on crutches*, nonetheless. I didn't know her name. I didn't need to. She ran into my heart and my life, and my mission suddenly became real.

I was a college junior, majoring in education, and was doing one of many field studies assigned in educational psychology. Baseline observations they were called. No emotions, just report the observations, the facts, the movements, patterns, and activity of this one cerebral palsy student in her teens.

I totally failed that day.

I could not be detached from the situation, as the assignment called for. I could not be objective or dispassionate. My soul had awakened from the slumber of my life.

You see this young *teenage girl,* who I had *not met* before this moment, dropped her crutches as she approached me and surrounded me with a hug. A stunning hug, a hug so real it would change my life. I could not describe the feelings rushing into me. Her joyful spirit was swallowing me up, and my new spirit was rising.

Finally, she let go of me, and her eyes became magnets to mine. The light of the Lord shone from her eyes and her smile. Knowing & trusting, it seemed that she knew *I was there for her*, and *she was there for me.*

Her name was Nancy, and she was there to give my heart guidance.

That day, I changed from an education major to a special education major. This one event began an eleven-year journey into teaching students with multiple disabilities. I was about to become who I was destined to be. I finally knew my calling, and my life would never be the same.

I surrendered to the moment, to this young girl who represented a world within our world, a neglected people. She had opened my heart with her smile and awakened a new beginning hiding in my soul. She was the door God wanted me to walk through, and on that journey, I met Him in each and every one of His people less noticed.

As I look back on a career of almost fifty years, working with students of all ages and abilities, I will always remember this young angel and how she opened my heart to a new path that not even the poets could describe.

Terry Focht

I hear your secrets, old heart.

WHO WE ARE

There is
the person
we think we are,

the person
other people
think we are,

the person
we think
other people
think we are,

finally,

there is
the person
God thinks we are.

I wonder which one
truly matters?

Let me see what I might be.

Special Recognition to:
The Thomas More University Creative Writing Vision Program

The Writers Table

Draft To Craft

Southern Appalachian Writers Cooperative

Poetry Night at Sitwell's

Wright Library Poets

Dayton Poetry Slam

A very special thanks to:
Sherry Cook Stanforth

Pauletta Hansel

Richard Hague

Chuck Stringer

John Cruze

Dick Westheimer

Erica Manto Paulson

Janice Focht

Terrill Martinez

George Ella Lyon

Manuel Iris

Parrish Monk

Lindsey Prince

Tina Neyer

I pray,

I find the wind.

SPECIAL THANKS TO THESE PUBLICATIONS

The author wishes to express his appreciation to the editors and publishers of the journals, books and anthologies in which versions of poems and prose have appeared.

Dos Madres Press - " Blessed be the River"

Pine Mountain Sand and Gravel - "Flat Footed Dancing and Turning in a Circle" and "Rustbelt Kid"

Words - "I Must Run" and "Those Crazy Dinosaurs"

The Dayton Anthology - "We Ran Into the Future Like We Knew the Way"

I Thought I Heard A Cardinal Sing, Anthology of Ohio Appalachian Voices - "Big Turtle Creek"

Mock Turtle Zine - "The Light" and "Deep Sorrow"

Kentucky Arts Council - "I Am From"

A River of Poems - "We Are From"

The Cincinnati Poet Laureates National Poetry Month - "Old Heart"

The University of Kentucky Permanent Special Collection - "We Are From" (Kentucky Voice)

Cincinnati Historical Museum Permanent Special Collection - "Fractured Reality"

Why We Write – "The Word Whisperer"

Additional selected versions or pieces from the author's previous books, *Random Acts of Thought* and *Grandpa Street*, appear in *I Hope I Find the Wind*.

ABOUT THE AUTHOR

Terry Focht has led a long career as both an educator and a professional in the field of education, working with students of all ages throughout his forty-three-year career. These experiences have helped shape his unique view of the world. He is a great observer of people and has been a lover of words, and intrigued by the power they hold, since he was a child.

Upon his retirement, he decided to devote his time to his poetry and prose as well as children's books for his granddaughters. He is a husband, a father, and a grandfather. He has seen and done much in his time here. Having lived in seven different states, he is "a man of many miles," who has traveled down many roads, on a journey that has been challenging, but often filled with grace and joy.

He is the author of *Random Acts of Thought* published in 2016 and a children's book, *Grandpa Street,* in 2020.

His stories and poems can be seen in:

Dos Madres Press

Why We Write

Pine Mountain Sand and Gravel

I Thought I Heard A Cardinal Sing, Anthology of Ohio Appalachian Voices

Words

The Dayton Anthology

Mock Turtle Zine

A River of Poems

Kentucky Arts Council

Ohio Arts Council

The Cincinnati Poet Laureates National Poetry Month

The Cincinnati Historical Museum Permanent Special Collection

The University of Kentucky Permanent Special Collection

Terry currently lives in Centerville, Ohio, with his wife Jan of fifty-five years, a talented artist to whom this book is dedicated.

OTHER BOOKS BY THE AUTHOR

Random *Acts of Thought*: This is Terry Focht's first poetry collection, published in 2016, by Bellamy-Fleming Publishing. It includes poems such as "Soul Birth," "Reflections," "A Child's Prayer," and "Reality of Fantasy." It's divided into seven sections: "Searching," "Growing," "Grace," "Joy," "Vision," "Heart," and "Blessed."

"*Random Acts of Thought* by Terry Focht is an easy, comfortable read and a book I will pick up again and again. A great gift idea for the contemplative reader." ~ Dianne, 5-star review on Amazon

Grandpa *Street:* In this picture book with illustrations by Lindsay Prince (2020, Braughler Books LLC), *Grandpa Street* is sure to tickle the funny bone of children of all ages. It is based on the true-life fun times the author shares with his granddaughters. It is the story of a silly, crazy grandpa that has many funny adventures with his granddaughters that he refers to as "Wiggle" and "Giggle." *Grandpa Street* is the first book in his *Wiggle and Giggle* seven book series.

"I bought this book as a gift for my great niece and nephew. The colors are vivid and bright with illustrations that add to the humor of each poem. The poems are sweet, amusing, and lyrical. I know my niece and nephew are going to love this book!" ~Amazon customer, 5-star review

ABOUT THE PUBLISHER

Editor-911 Books is a traditional, independent publisher, owned by Margo L. Dill, in St. Louis, Missouri, that specializes in children's books, fiction for young adults and adults and books that don't always fit the mold of what's been previously published, such as this beautiful book you just read by Terry Focht. To find out more about Editor-911 Books and all of our offerings, check out our website at www.Editor-911.com. We are in business to bring books to readers from talented authors who also don't always fit the norm. Each book in our various imprints is carefully selected and sculpted into what you see today. Check them out anywhere books are available!

"We publish books that readers love but aren't traditional. We're outside the box and happy to be here!"

OTHER BOOKS BY THE PUBLISHER
www.editor-911.com
Available where books are sold

Greenwood Gone: Henry's Story by Sioux Roslawski (historical fiction for ages 9-12): Greenwood District, Oklahoma, 1921: Twelve-year-old Henry Simmons has lived his entire life in Greenwood, Oklahoma, a district in the northern part of Tulsa. He's loved by his parents and neighbors, annoyed by his little sister, and protected by his community, a neighborhood full of hard-working, successful Black people like his mama and daddy. People call Greenwood "Black Wall Street," and Henry plans to grow up there until he becomes a famous writer or baseball player—or both.

Sure, he sees racism firsthand when he goes with his daddy to "White Tulsa." But for most of his life, as long as his friends and neighbors stay in Greenwood, the White folks of Tulsa don't cause too much trouble in Henry's life.

Until May 31, 1921.

That's the night Henry's life changes forever. His family's life changes forever. All the neighborhoods of Greenwood change forever—because 19-year-old Dick Rowland, a Black shoeshiner working in Tulsa, is accused of assaulting a White female elevator operator. That accusation and Dick's arrest turn into twelve hours of terror for Greenwood residents. And Henry and his family are right in the middle of the chaos, hate, and massacre.

For these twelve hours, Henry, his mother, and his younger sister Livvie watch White men and women destroy their neighborhood while they miss Daddy, who went to help protect Dick at the courthouse. Sometimes, Henry, Mama, and Livvie hide; sometimes, they flee; and always, they are shocked by the terrifying behavior of their fellow human beings.

"I realize this book is written for children. I'm an adult; Henry's story gripped my heart and soul and gave me a new perspective. This book is more than a worthwhile story for any mature age group." ~Amazon customer, 5-star review

"Fast-paced and honest, *Greenwood Gone: Henry's Story* is one of THE ways to peak the interest of middle school students and share with them an important, and devastating, life- and landscape-changing event not found in school history books. Told from the point of view of 12-year-old Henry Simmons, *Greenwood Gone* aims to give readers a glimpse of the horrifying racism that existed in the 1921; yet the same story could have been told in 2021. In addition to recounting the horrendous bullying, killing and destroying of the Black residents of Greenwood, Oklahoma, Henry's story shows the strength and perseverance of Black families and the unexpected kindness of strangers. My favorite part of the story is near the end when Henry reveals that he became interested in writing because of his English teacher, Mrs. Murray. In real life, I know Mrs. Murray was the BEST of the best teachers. Read this book, then read about Greenwood, then order a class set for your students!" ~Joe, 5-star Amazon review

The Earth Loves Me by Terrill Martinez (daughter of Terry Focht!) with illustrations by Elsa Escoto: "The Earth loves me, and the Earth loves you too." This book honors the wonderful natural elements of Earth, from tall mountains to low valleys, from oceans to fields of flowers and the animals that live here too. The child in this book marvels at the gifts nature offers her and the fun she can have in it: the wind whispers secrets, the grass tickles her feet, and the flowers remind her that life is sweet. Terrill Martinez's poetic words about the Earth we love, and that loves us back, come to life in the beautiful and colorful illustrations from talented artist and illustrator Elsa Escoto.

This book is perfect for Earth Day, habitat studies, and environmental talks and incorporates poetic language to celebrate the beautiful Earth, every day of our lives. It's a wonderful book for any parent to read to their children or teacher to a class and includes an educational activity for home or classroom.

The Earth Loves Me by Terrill Martinez will foster in your child a love for and an appreciation of the miraculous gifts our amazing planet offers to us all.

"A beautifully written and illustrated book about loving our Earth as it loves us. The author thoughtfully reminds us all (big and small) of what the Earth provides for us. I bought several to share with my boys, my niece and nephew and friends." ~5-star review, Amazon customer

"*The Earth Loves Me* introduces the youngest readers to the overwhelming beauty of the earth. Kids will relate to many of the activities, like walking in the rain and making snow angels. I can picture parents and teachers reading this book outdoors, so kids can feel the grass beneath their feet and the wind on their faces." ~Kristine Zimmerman, Readers' Favorite

For a complete list of Editor-911 Books, check out our website, Editor-911.com.

Perhaps…there is a destiny for words.

Made in the USA
Coppell, TX
12 March 2024

29933609R00056